DEC 0 4 2008

GLENDALE CALIF. PUBLIC LIBRARY 91205

CHEVY CHASE

NO LONGER PROPERTY OF
GLENDALE   LIBRARY
ARTS & CULTURE DEPT.

D0933756

DEC 0 4 2008

Why Things Don't Work
TRAIN

Published by Raintree, a division of Reed Elsevier, Inc.
Chicago, Illinois

Customer Service 888-363-4266
Visit our website at www.raintreelibrary.com

Why Things Don't Work TRAIN
was produced by

David West ⚇ Children's Books
7 Princeton Court
55 Felsham Road
London SW15 1AZ

Editor: Dominique Crowley
Consultant: David T. Wright

Copyright © 2007 David West Children's Books

All rights reserved. No part of this publication may be reproduced or transmitted
in any form or by any means, electronic, mechanical, including photocopying, recording, taping,
or any information storage and retrieval system without permission in writing
from the Publisher: Raintree, 100 N. LaSalle, Suite 1200, Chicago, IL 60602

11 10 09 08 07
10 9 8 7 6 5 4 3 2 1

Library of Congress Cataloging-in-Publication Data

West, David.
  Train / by David West.
      p. cm. -- (Why things don't work)
  Includes index.
  ISBN 1-4109-2557-9
  1. Railroads--Trains--Juvenile literature. I. Title.
  TF148.W47 2006
  625.1--dc22
                                        2006020399

Printed and bound in China

Why Things Don't Work

TRAIN

by David West

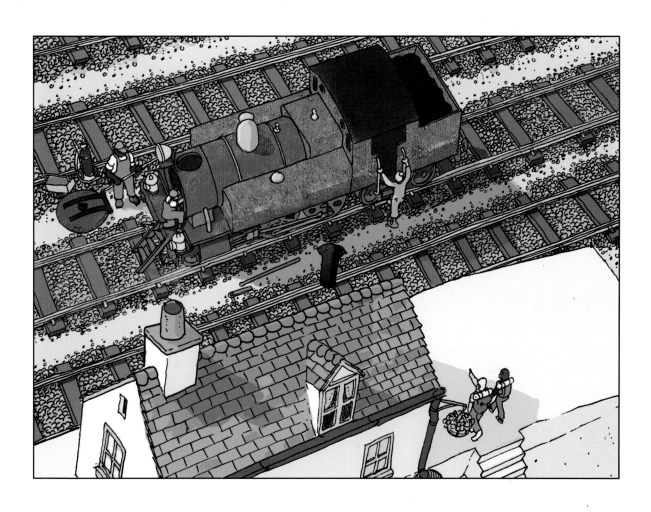

Raintree
Chicago, Illinois

J
625.1
WES

Contents

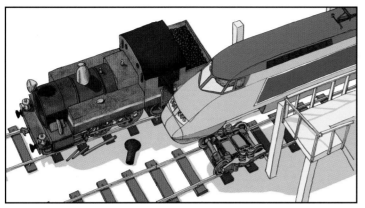

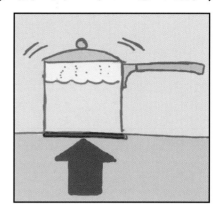
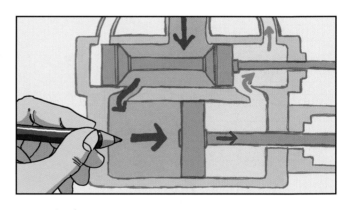
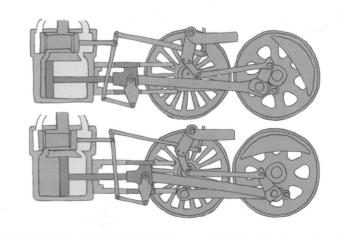

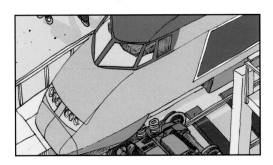

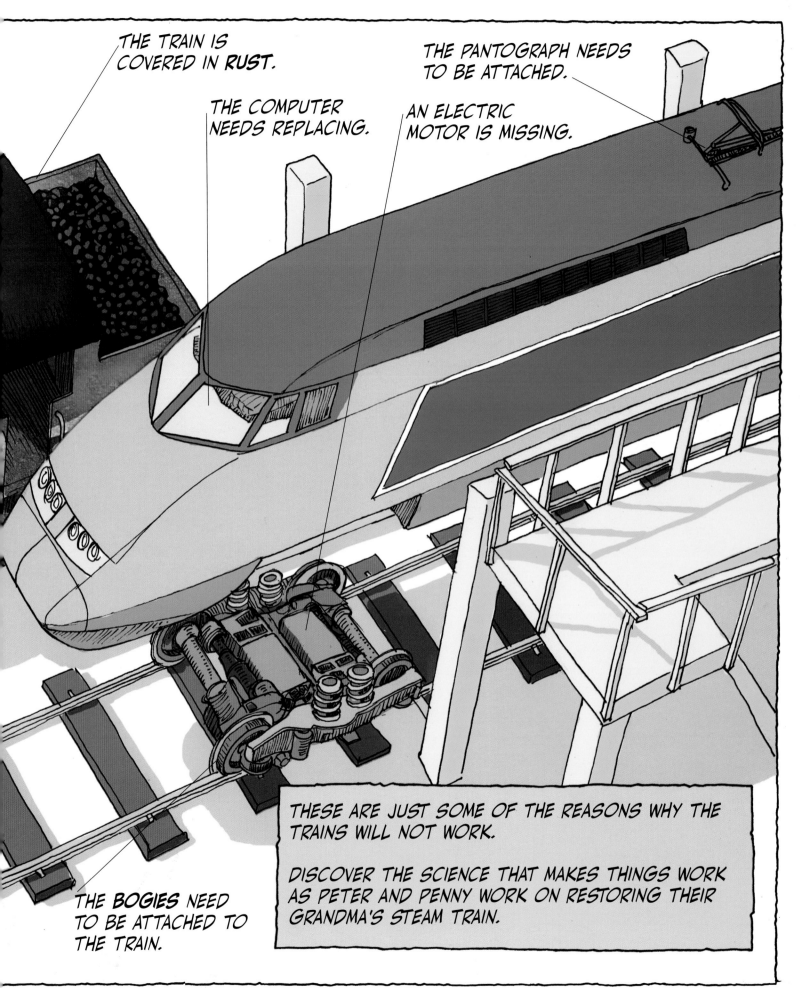

PETER AND PENNY ARRIVE AT GRANDMA'S TRAIN MUSEUM.

WOW! THIS PLACE IS GREAT!

THERE'S GRANDMA LIZZIE.

OVER HERE, KIDS.

YOU'VE ARRIVED JUST IN TIME TO HELP WITH MY TANK ENGINE.

LET'S PUT YOUR BAGS IN THE STATION HOUSE.

WHY IS YOUR TRAIN CALLED A TANK ENGINE, GRANDMA?

BECAUSE IT'S GOT WATER TANKS ON THE SIDE OF THE ENGINE.

DOES THE WATER KEEP IT COOL?

NO. YOU NEED LOTS OF WATER TO MAKE THIS ENGINE WORK.

WHAT DO YOU GET WHEN YOU HEAT WATER?

STEAM?

REEEEEP

THAT'S RIGHT, STEAM! THIS TRAIN USES STEAM TO RUN ITS ENGINE.

HOW DOES THE TRAIN MAKE THE STEAM?

FOLLOW ME AND I'LL SHOW YOU.

INSIDE THAT LONG CYLINDER IS THE BOILER.

THIS IS THE SMOKEBOX. BEHIND IT IS THE BOILER'S WATER TANK.

WHAT ARE ALL THOSE HOLES?

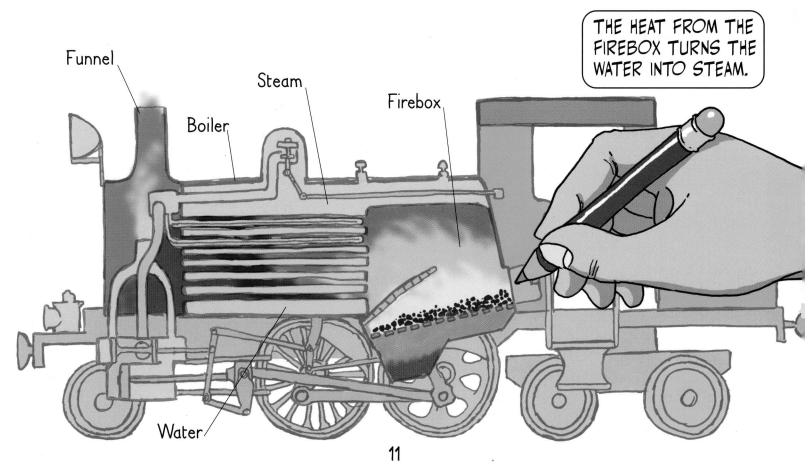

11

12

AS THE WATER TURNS INTO STEAM, IT BUILDS UP PRESSURE.

THIS IS BECAUSE STEAM (A GAS) TAKES UP MORE SPACE THAN WATER (A LIQUID).

Steam

Boiling water (212°F)

Heat

BUT THE STEAM CANNOT EXPAND UNTIL IT HAS BUILT UP ENOUGH PRESSURE. THEN, IT HAS THE POWER TO MOVE THINGS, JUST LIKE THE LID OFF A SAUCEPAN.

Steam

Boiling water

Heat

THIS GAUGE, HERE, SHOWS THE PRESSURE. WHEN THE STEAM GETS TO A HIGH ENOUGH PRESSURE, IT CAN BE PIPED TO THE PISTONS.

YOU CAN SEE THE PISTONS AT THE FRONT. THERE IS ONE SET ON EACH SIDE OF THE TRAIN.

AS YOU CAN SEE, THERE ARE TWO PISTONS IN EACH **CYLINDER** CASING.

HOW DO THEY WORK?

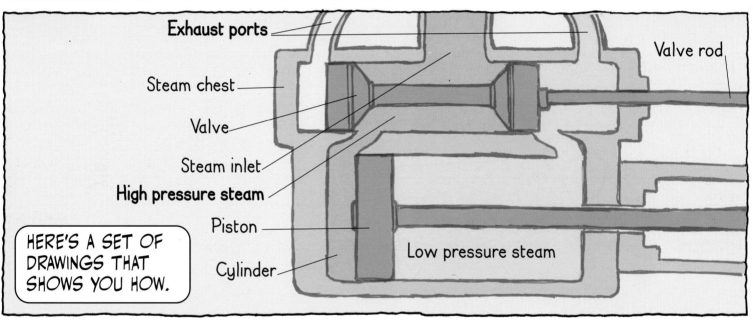

Exhaust ports

Steam chest

Valve

Steam inlet

High pressure steam

Piston

Cylinder

Valve rod

Low pressure steam

HERE'S A SET OF DRAWINGS THAT SHOWS YOU HOW.

HIGH PRESSURE STEAM FROM THE BOILER ENTERS THE CYLINDER THROUGH THE INLET. AS IT EXPANDS IT PUSHES THE PISTON.

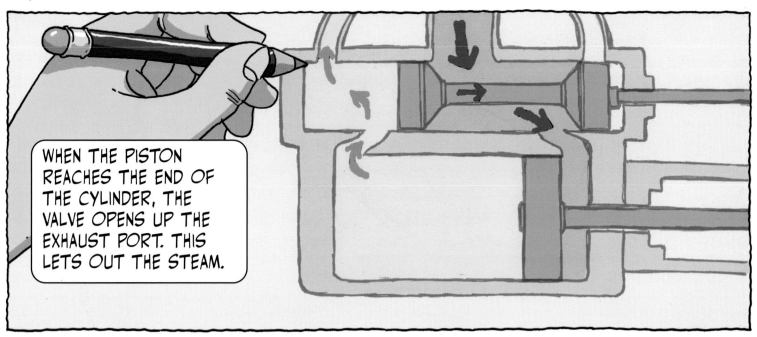

WHEN THE PISTON REACHES THE END OF THE CYLINDER, THE VALVE OPENS UP THE EXHAUST PORT. THIS LETS OUT THE STEAM.

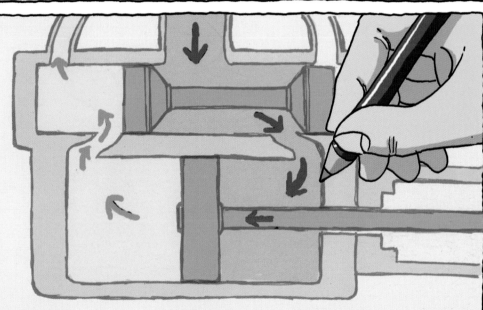

THE VALVE ALSO ALLOWS HIGH PRESSURE STEAM TO ENTER FROM THE RIGHT. THIS PUSHES THE PISTON TO THE OTHER END OF THE CYLINDER.

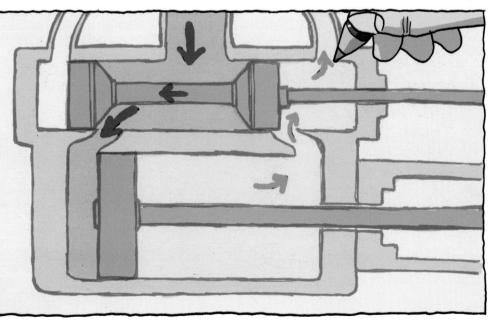

WHEN THE PISTON REACHES THE END OF THE CYLINDER, THE VALVE OPENS UP THE EXHAUST PORT ON THE OTHER SIDE TO ALLOW THE EXPANDED STEAM OUT. THEN, THE WHOLE PROCESS IS READY TO START AGAIN.

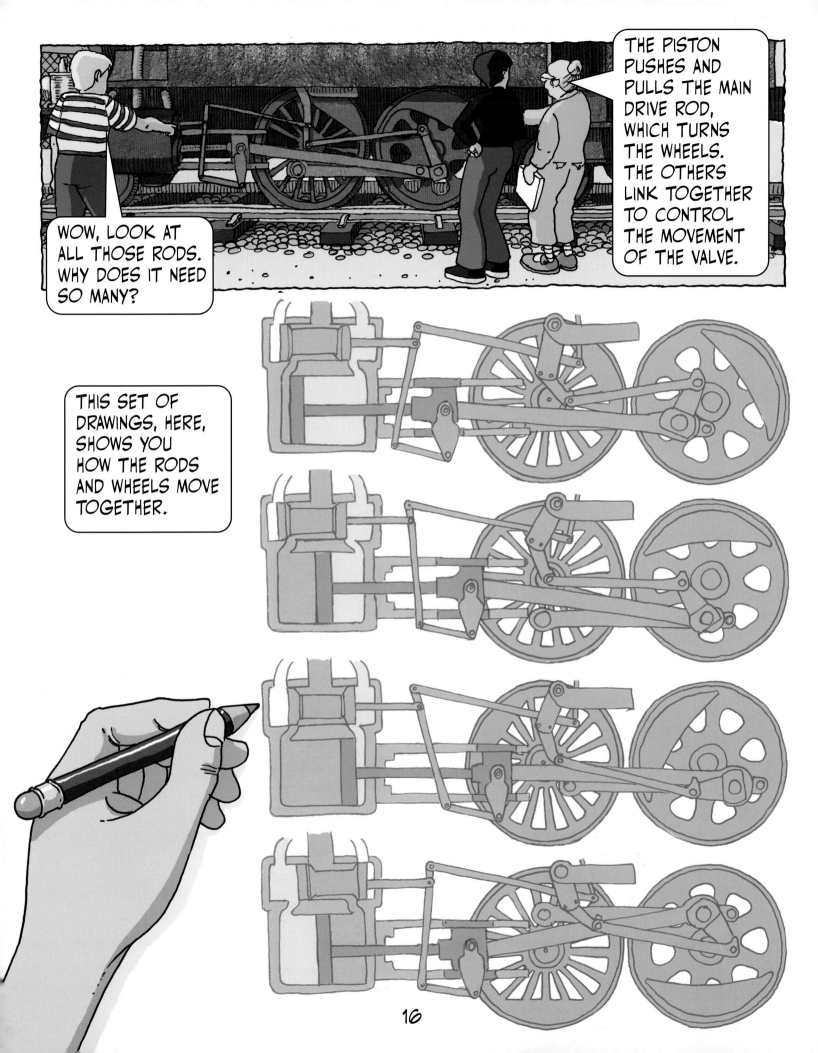

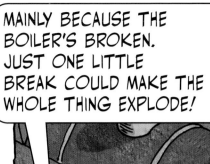

WHY DOESN'T THE TRAIN WORK, GRANDMA?

MAINLY BECAUSE THE BOILER'S BROKEN. JUST ONE LITTLE BREAK COULD MAKE THE WHOLE THING EXPLODE!

EVEN WHEN THIS TRAIN WAS RUNNING IN THE FIRST HALF OF THE TWENTIETH CENTURY, IT WOULD NEED TO HAVE THE BOILER REPAIRED EVERY FIVE YEARS.

WE'RE ALMOST DONE, NOW.

WHAT ARE THOSE PIPES FOR?

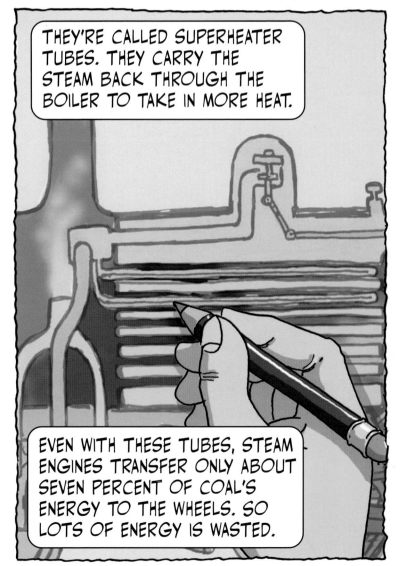

THEY'RE CALLED SUPERHEATER TUBES. THEY CARRY THE STEAM BACK THROUGH THE BOILER TO TAKE IN MORE HEAT.

EVEN WITH THESE TUBES, STEAM ENGINES TRANSFER ONLY ABOUT SEVEN PERCENT OF COAL'S ENERGY TO THE WHEELS. SO LOTS OF ENERGY IS WASTED.

WHAT IS THIS PIPE, HERE?

THAT'S WHERE THE SPENT STEAM FROM THE PISTONS' EXHAUST PORT COMES OUT.

THE STEAM SHOOTING UPWARD HELPS DRAW THE SMOKE WITH IT. THAT'S WHERE THE "CHUFF-CHUFF" SOUND COMES FROM.

BY THE END OF THE WEEK, THE TANK ENGINE WAS FINISHED.

THE BOILER HAD BEEN COMPLETELY REPAIRED.

THE PISTONS HAD BEEN CLEANED AND PUT BACK TOGETHER.

THE SMOKEBOX DOOR HAD BEEN FIXED BACK ON.

THE CHIMNEY HAD BEEN FITTED.

AND ALL THE RODS HAD BEEN OILED AND PUT BACK ON.

FINALLY, WE CLEANED THE RUST OFF THE ENTIRE TRAIN...

WHERE DOES RUST COME FROM?

IT'S A CHEMICAL REACTION CALLED **OXIDIZATION**, WHEN OXYGEN IN THE DAMP AIR REACTS WITH THE IRON.

AND PAINTED IT.

PAINTING THE METAL HELPS PROTECT IT FROM RUSTING.

THE NEXT MORNING...

LOOK. THERE'S SMOKE COMING FROM THE FUNNEL.

HI, KIDS. CLIMB UP ON THE FOOTPLATE. WE'RE BUILDING UP STEAM FOR A TEST RUN!

SHOVEL SOME MORE COAL IN, PETER.

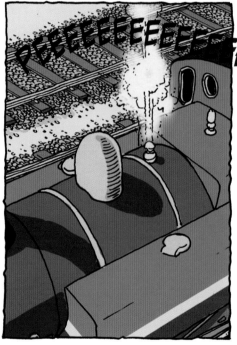

PEEEEEEEEEP

THE SAFETY VALVE IS STUCK OPEN.

IF TOO MUCH PRESSURE BUILDS UP THIS VALVE OPENS TO LET OFF STEAM.

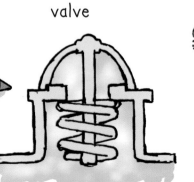

valve

Steam

High pressure steam

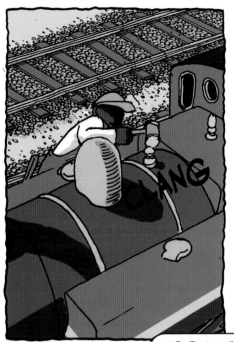

THAT'S FIXED IT! GREAT!

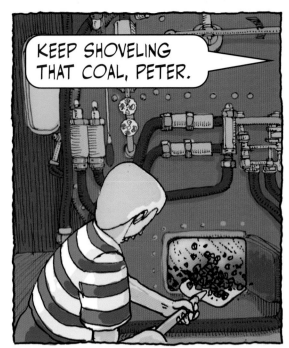

KEEP SHOVELING THAT COAL, PETER.

LOOK. THE PRESSURE GAUGE SHOWS WE HAVE ENOUGH PRESSURE TO START.

OK, PENNY, RELEASE THAT BRAKE LEVER.

PETER, PULL THE **THROTTLE LEVER**, THERE.

THAT OPENS THE THROTTLE VALVE IN THE STEAM DOME, WHICH LETS THE STEAM THROUGH TO THE PISTONS.

Steam dome

Throttle valve

22

A HALF HOUR LATER...

WE NEED TO STOP NOW AND HEAD BACK.

HOW DO WE TURN AROUND?

CRANK

WE DON'T NEED TO. WE JUST REVERSE THE WHEELS BY PULLING ON THAT LEVER.

THE ENGINE STARTED TO GO BACKWARD.

BACK AT THE TRAIN MUSEUM'S STATION...

THAT WAS COOL!

IF YOU THINK THAT WAS COOL, COME AND SEE MY NEW ADDITION.

WOW! WHAT IS IT?

IT'S A FRENCH HIGH-SPEED ELECTRIC TRAIN CALLED A TGV.

23

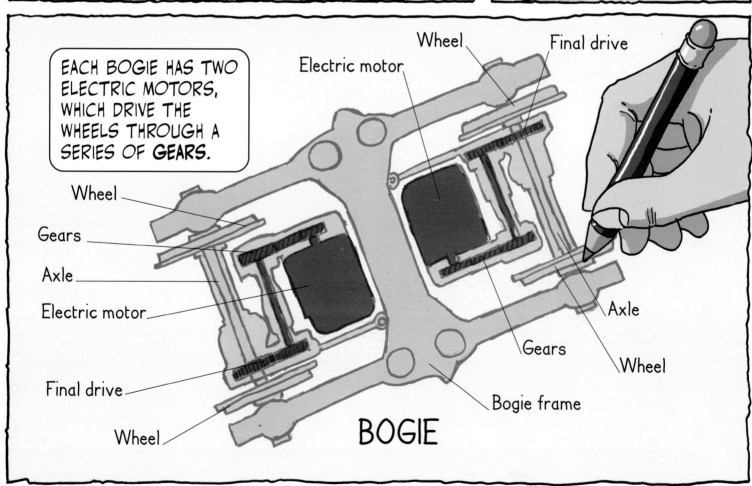

BOGIE

24

HOW DO ELECTRIC MOTORS WORK?

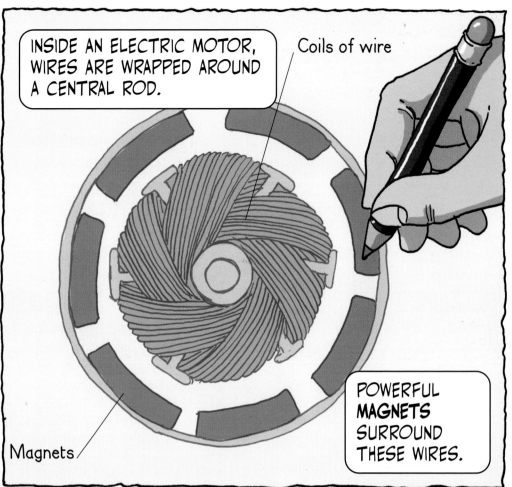

INSIDE AN ELECTRIC MOTOR, WIRES ARE WRAPPED AROUND A CENTRAL ROD.

Coils of wire

Magnets

POWERFUL **MAGNETS** SURROUND THESE WIRES.

WHEN ELECTRICITY PASSES THROUGH THE COILS OF WIRE, THEY CREATE A MAGNETIC FIELD OPPOSITE TO THOSE OF THE MAGNETS.

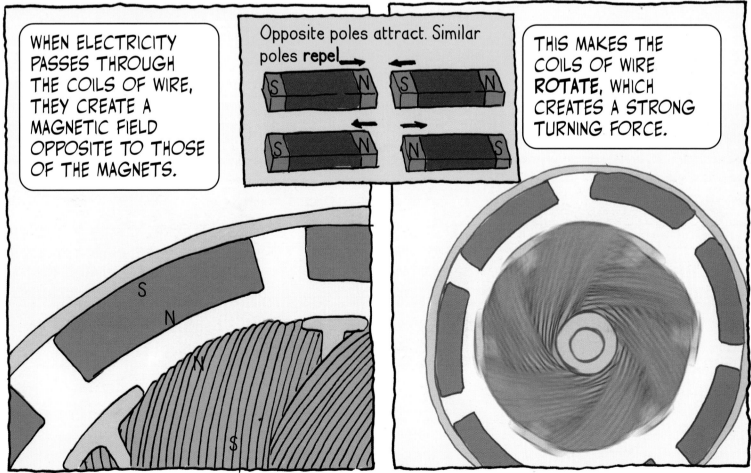

Opposite poles attract. Similar poles **repel**

THIS MAKES THE COILS OF WIRE **ROTATE**, WHICH CREATES A STRONG TURNING FORCE.

WHERE DOES THE TRAIN GET ITS ELECTRICITY FROM?

FROM AN OVERHEAD ELECTRICAL WIRE. THE TRAIN HAS A DEVICE CALLED A PANTOGRAPH, WHICH PICKS UP THE ELECTRICITY FROM THE OVERHEAD WIRE. THE ELECTRICAL CURRENT PASSES THROUGH A TRANSFORMER AND THEN TO THE MOTORS.

WHAT'S A TRANSFORMER?

ELECTRICITY IN THE OVERHEAD WIRE IS AT A VERY HIGH VOLTAGE. THE MOTORS USE A LOWER VOLTAGE. THE TRAIN HAS A TRANSFORMER TO CHANGE THE VOLTAGE SO THE MOTORS CAN USE IT. THIS DIAGRAM SHOWS HOW A TRANSFORMER WORKS.

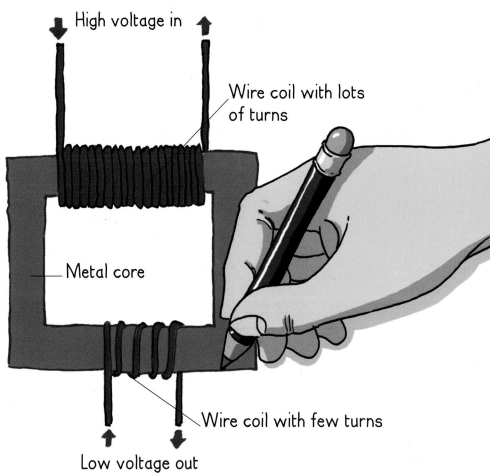

High voltage in

Wire coil with lots of turns

Metal core

Wire coil with few turns

Low voltage out

WHEN WILL YOU HAVE IT FIXED?

VERY SOON. WE'RE JUST WAITING FOR A NEW COMPUTER.

WHY DOES IT NEED A COMPUTER?

ALL THE DIFFERENT SYSTEMS, FROM BRAKES TO ELECTRICAL SUPPLY, NEED TO BE MONITORED AND CONTROLLED. THE **COMPUTER** DOES THIS, SO THE DRIVER CAN CONCENTRATE ON DRIVING THE TRAIN.

THE NEXT DAY, PETER AND PENNY LOOKED AROUND THE TRAIN MUSEUM.

THIS IS A **REPLICA** OF THE FIRST EVER STEAM TRAIN. IT WAS BUILT BY TREVITHICK IN 1803.

THIS ONE HAS A DEVICE ON THE FRONT CALLED A COW CATCHER.

LOOK AT THIS PICTURE OF BIG BOY. THIS WAS THE BIGGEST STEAM TRAIN EVER BUILT.

28

THIS IS THE MALLARD. IT WAS BUILT IN 1938 AND DESIGNED BY SIR NIGEL GRESLEY. IT STILL HOLDS THE RECORD FOR THE FASTEST STEAM TRAIN AT 126 MILES PER HOUR.

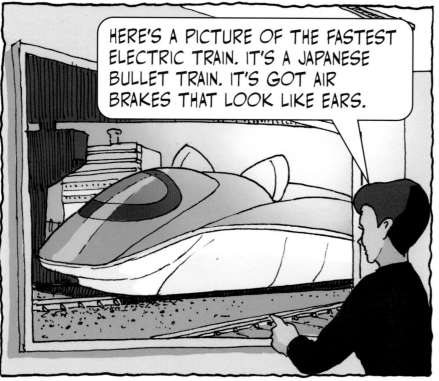

HERE'S A PICTURE OF THE FASTEST ELECTRIC TRAIN. IT'S A JAPANESE BULLET TRAIN. IT'S GOT AIR BRAKES THAT LOOK LIKE EARS.

HERE'S A PICTURE OF A TRAIN THAT HOVERS ON MAGNETS! IT'S CALLED A MAGLEV TRAIN.

FINALLY IT WAS TIME TO GO. GRANDMA DROPPED PETER AND PENNY AT THE TRAIN STATION.

THANKS FOR HELPING ME OUT, KIDS. I'LL LET YOU KNOW WHEN THE TGV IS READY.

LOOK! IT'S THE SAME TRAIN AS GRANDMA'S!

29

Parts of a Steam Train

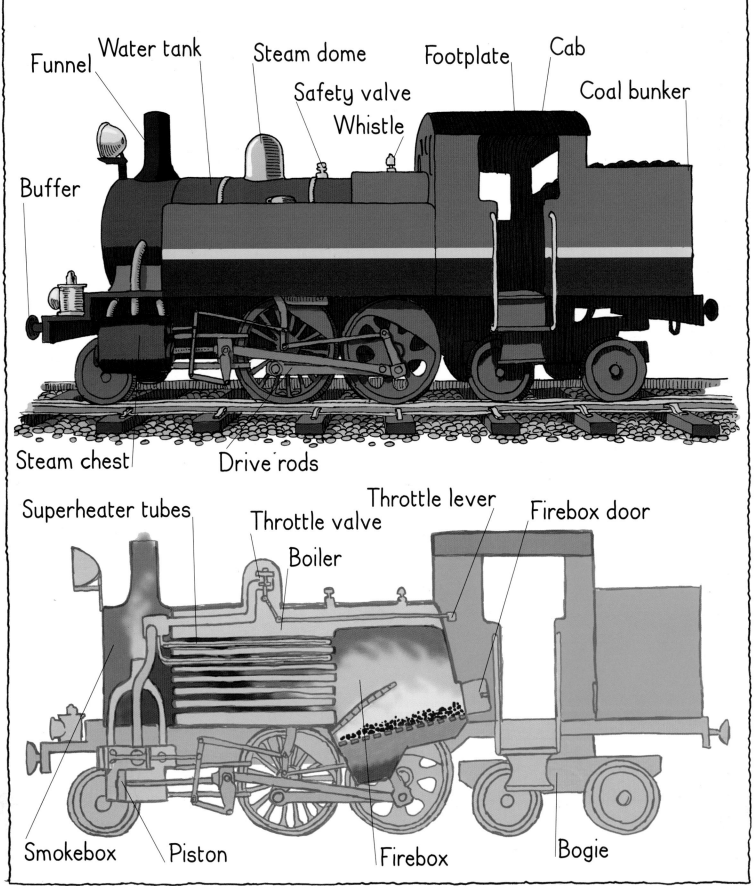

Funnel
Water tank
Steam dome
Footplate
Cab
Safety valve
Whistle
Coal bunker
Buffer
Steam chest
Drive rods
Superheater tubes
Throttle lever
Throttle valve
Firebox door
Boiler
Smokebox
Piston
Firebox
Bogie

Glossary

BOGIE
FRAME WITH FOUR WHEELS THAT
SUPPORTS THE TRAIN

BOILER
METAL CONTAINER HOLDING WATER THAT
IS TURNED INTO STEAM

COAL BUNKER
PLACE WHERE THE COAL IS STORED

COMPUTER
ELECTRONIC DEVICE THAT CAN BE
PROGRAMMED TO CONTROL THE VARIOUS
WORKINGS OF A MACHINE

CYLINDER
METAL SLEEVE INSIDE WHICH A
PISTON MOVES

DRIVE RODS
METAL RODS ATTACHED TO THE PISTONS
AND THE WHEELS, WHICH TURN
THE WHEELS

EXHAUST PORT
HOLES IN THE STEAM CHEST THROUGH
WHICH THE EXPANDED STEAM EXITS

FIREBOX
PLACE, INSIDE A STEAM TRAIN, WHERE THE
COAL IS BURNED

GEARS
A SET OF WHEELS THAT TRANSFER
POWER. THE WHEELS HAVE TEETH ON
THEIR RIM, WHICH ALLOWS THEM TO
GRIP EACH OTHER.

HIGH PRESSURE STEAM
STEAM THAT IS VERY HOT AND HAS NOT
BEEN ALLOWED TO EXPAND

MAGNET
A PIECE OF METAL, USUALLY IRON, WHICH
HAS A MAGNETIC FIELD WITH NORTH AND
SOUTH POLES

OXIDIZATION
THE PROCESS OF RUSTING, WHEN A
METAL, SUCH AS IRON, REACTS WITH
OXYGEN IN A DAMP ATMOSPHERE

PISTON
A SOLID CYLINDER THAT MOVES BACK AND
FORTH INSIDE ANOTHER CYLINDER

REPEL
TO FORCE AWAY

REPLICA
A COPY

ROTATE
TURN

RUST
THE RESULT OF OXYDIZATION

THROTTLE LEVER
CONTROL THAT MAKES THE TRAIN SPEED
UP OR SLOW DOWN

VALVE
A DEVICE THAT OPENS AND CLOSES,
ALLOWING A GAS OR LIQUID THROUGH AN
OPENING—USUALLY ONLY ONE WAY

Index